creatures
of the sea

Beluga Whales

Other titles in the series:

creatures of the sea

Beluga Whales

Kris Hirschmann

**KIDHAVEN
PRESS**™

THOMSON
━━━━✦━━━━™
GALE

San Diego • Detroit • New York • San Francisco • Cleveland
New Haven, Conn. • Waterville, Maine • London • Munich

© 2004 by KidHaven Press. KidHaven Press is an imprint of The Gale Group, Inc.,
a division of Thomson Learning, Inc.

KidHaven™ and Thomson Learning™ are trademarks used herein under license.

For more information, contact
KidHaven Press
27500 Drake Rd.
Farmington Hills, MI 48331-3535
Or you can visit our Internet site at http://www.gale.com

LIBRARY OF CONGRESS CATALOGING-IN-PUBLICATION DATA

Hirschmann, Kris, 1967–
  Beluga whales / By Kristine Hirschmann.
    p. cm.—(Creatures of the sea)
Summary: Describes the physical characteristics, behavior, life cyle,and habitat of
beluga whales.
Includes bibliographical references and index.
  ISBN 0-7377-1553-7 (hardback : alk. paper)
  1. White whale—Juvenile literature. [1. White whale. 2. Whales.] I.Title.
  QL737.C433H57 2004
  599.5'42—dc21

                                                        2003007297

Printed in China

Table of contents

Finding Belugas

Beluga whales are often found in aquariums. Marine parks around the world keep these animals on display. There are several reasons for this. Belugas are small compared to most whales. This makes them easy to keep in captivity. In addition, beluga whales are attractive. Their mouths seem to be smiling, their snow-white skin is pleasing to the eye, and their rounded foreheads give them an amusing look. Belugas are also smart and can be taught to do tricks. For all of these reasons, people tend to enjoy beluga whales and to see them as gentle, friendly creatures.

This impression is not an illusion. Belugas really are gentle and friendly. Wild beluga whales are curious about people and often approach boats. They sometimes swim up to divers and circle them with interest before swimming away. People who often dive in the same area can even make friends

The beluga whale's upturned mouth gives the impression that the whale is always smiling.

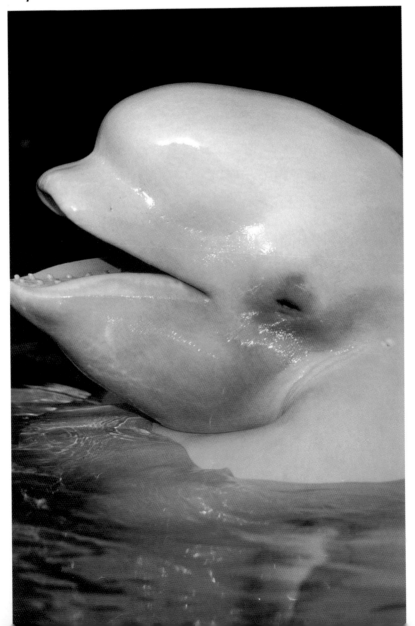

with the local beluga whales. A loud clap or another noise attracts the whales' attention. The belugas then swim over to greet the familiar diver.

Finding wild beluga whales, however, is not always easy. During the summer, belugas live in remote areas of the Arctic. At this time, belugas are so far from where most people live that they are difficult to watch or study. Some scientists use helicopters and boats to track belugas into the far north. But most wait for the belugas to travel south for the winter. During these months, belugas are most likely to come in contact with humans.

Still, most people do not want to dive into the water in the middle of the winter, when belugas are near. Therefore, only a few people get the opportunity to swim with wild beluga whales. But this does not matter. Aquariums let people everywhere see the beluga's happy grin. And as long as belugas keep smiling, they will keep their reputation as the world's friendliest whales.

The White Whale

Beluga whales belong to the scientific order Cetacea, which includes all whales, dolphins, and porpoises. Within this order, belugas are included in the subgroup *Odontoceti*, which means toothed whales. The toothed whale group also includes killer whales, beaked whales, narwhals, sperm whales, dolphins, and porpoises.

The beluga's scientific name is *Delphinapterus leucas*, which is Latin for "white dolphin without a fin." The beluga gets this name from its color, its dolphinlike shape, and its finless back.

The Beluga Body

As whales go, belugas are on the small side. Adult male belugas measure between eleven and fifteen feet in length and weigh up to thirty-three hundred pounds. Females are smaller, measuring ten to thirteen feet in length and weighing up to three thousand pounds. The bodies of both males and females are stocky and have rolls of fat along the bottom surface.

Belugas have distinctive heads with high, rounded foreheads and small beaks. The beak opening is the beluga's mouth. The mouth curves upward at the ends. This creates a permanent "grin" on the beluga's face.

At the back of the head is the whale's neck. The beluga is the only whale with neck bones that are

The beluga's sloping forehead and curved mouth give it a dolphinlike appearance.

not joined together. For this reason, belugas' necks are much more flexible than those of other whales. A beluga can turn its head from side to side and nod it up and down. It is the only whale that can make these motions.

Just behind the beluga's head are two small, rounded flippers that curl up at the tips. These flippers are attached near the bottom of the body and stick out on both sides. They are used to keep the whale stable in the water as it swims.

At the rear of the beluga's body is a powerful tail ending in two lobes. Each lobe of the tail is called a fluke. The **flukes** are flattened pads of tough tissue. When a beluga waves its tail up and down, the flukes create pressure in the water and push the whale forward.

As its scientific name suggests, the beluga whale does not have a fin on its back. In the Arctic waters where the beluga whale makes its home, a dorsal, or back, fin might bump into floating ice chunks. This could be a problem for a traveling whale. So, instead of a fin, belugas have bumpy spines called **dorsal ridges** that run from the middle of the back all the way to the flukes. A beluga can use this hard ridge to break through ice as thick as three inches.

Thick White Skin

A beluga whale's skin is one of its most distinctive features. In adults, the skin is pure white during most of the year. During the summer, the skin may turn yellow along the back and flippers. This is a sign that a beluga is getting ready to **molt**, or shed the top layer of its skin. Belugas molt once a year, usually around July. They get rid of their old skin by turning upside down and rubbing their backs and flippers against gravelly ocean bottoms. This process scrapes off the dead material and brings fresh new skin to the surface of the whale's body.

Beluga skin is unusual not only because of its color. It is also extremely thick. Beluga whales have the thickest skin of any **cetacean** species. They are the only whales with skin thick enough to be made into leather.

Marine Mammals

Belugas are **marine mammals**. Like all mammals, beluga whales are warm-blooded. Belugas keep a constant internal temperature of around 98 or 99° Fahrenheit, about the same temperature that is normal in humans. Doing this can be difficult in the ice-filled waters where beluga whales make their home. For this reason, belugas have physical features that preserve their body heat in even the coldest water. They have a three-inch-thick layer of fat called **blubber** under their skin that protects the inner body from the cold. Also, a beluga's blood vessels can constrict, or get narrower, to keep blood away from the skin's surface when conditions are particularly chilly. This keeps valuable body heat from being lost to the environment.

Like other mammals, belugas also breathe air. A beluga breathes through a single hole on top of its head. This hole is called a **blowhole**. When the beluga is underwater, it holds its breath and covers the blowhole with a flap of skin. To breathe, the beluga surfaces and pushes the blowhole out of the water. It exhales, shooting a cloud of seawater and water vapor into the air. This cloud is called the **blow**, and

The beluga whale breathes through its blowhole.

it can shoot as high as three feet. After exhaling, the beluga sucks in new air. Then it closes the blowhole and goes back underwater.

Once underwater, the beluga whale can hold its breath as long as fifteen minutes. A diving beluga's heart rate slows from about one hundred beats per minute to less than twenty. This slowdown helps the whale to conserve oxygen so it can stay underwater longer.

Beluga Senses

Beluga whales spend a lot of time swimming beneath ice floes, where there is little light. In this

A beluga "spyhops" when it pokes its head from the water to see what is happening above the surface.

Anatomy of the Beluga Whale

A whale's blowhole allows the whale to breathe

Muscles in the rounded forehead of the whale help shape the sounds it produces

Fat in the beluga's lower jawbone picks up vibrations to help the whale hear

Two small, rounded flippers keep the whale balanced as it swims

The beluga waves its tail, made up of two wide flukes, to push forward in the water

environment, belugas depend on their sense of hearing to find their way around and locate other whales. Belugas have excellent hearing and can detect pitches about six times higher than the human ear can hear.

Belugas have two ear openings, one behind each eye. However, most scientists believe that these ear openings are not used to receive sounds. Instead, belugas hear with their jaws. A beluga whale's lower jawbone is filled with fat. This fat picks up sound vibrations and passes them to bones in the whale's inner ears. From there, sounds are sent to hearing centers in the brain.

Although they depend mostly on hearing, belugas also have good eyesight. Beluga whales can see well in both dim and bright light. Scientists believe they can probably see colors, too. And, unlike many marine animals, belugas can even see well through air. Beluga whales often briefly poke their heads out of the water to see what is going on above the surface. This behavior is called **"spyhopping."**

Other senses play a smaller role in the beluga's lifestyle. Belugas can touch and taste, but these senses are not thought to be important in the beluga's daily life. Smell is not important either. In fact, belugas may not be able to smell at all. Their brains do not seem to have parts that process smells, so scientists think that beluga whales probably lack this sense.

But a missing sense of smell does not seem to be a problem for beluga whales. These graceful animals have everything they need to thrive in their environment. From their snowy skins to their thick blubber and sharp senses, belugas truly are built for life in the ocean.

2

The Beluga Lifestyle

There are probably about eighty thousand beluga whales in the world. These whales are found only in the northern part of the globe. They live in the Arctic Ocean and its surrounding seas, including the Bering Sea, the Gulf of Alaska, and Canada's Hudson Bay. Sometimes they also enter rivers. Belugas are often seen hundreds of miles up the Amur River in Russia and the Yukon and St. Lawrence Rivers of Canada.

Wherever it lives, a healthy wild beluga whale lives about twenty-five to thirty years. During this lifetime, the whale follows a predictable yearly cycle. Autumn and spring are times for **migration**. Spring is also mating season, and summer brings baby belugas. The new babies soon learn about the beluga lifestyle. They will follow this lifestyle for the rest of their lives and pass it on to their own babies when the time comes.

Social Animals

Beluga whales are social animals. They live in stable groups called **pods**, which usually have about ten members. Sometimes pods join together to form larger groups. Herds of up to ten thousand belugas have been seen. But large herds like this are temporary and usually break up quickly.

A pod of beluga whales contains both males and females and is usually led by one large male. Female belugas with babies form separate nursery pods.

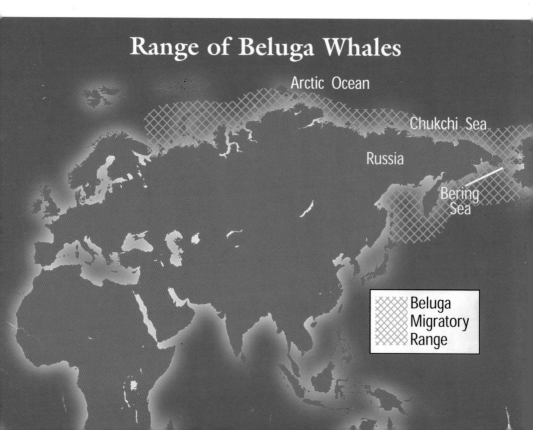

Range of Beluga Whales

Arctic Ocean

Chukchi Sea

Russia

Bering Sea

Beluga Migratory Range

The members of a pod move from place to place as a group. As they travel, they play by chasing each other and rubbing against each other. They often swim side by side, breaking the surface at the same time to breathe.

Different Homes

During the winter months, when much of the Arctic Ocean is covered by ice, beluga pods are found at the southern ends of their range. Winter homes include the coast of Alaska in the Bering Sea, the southern coast of Hudson Bay, and the southwestern coast of Greenland. Belugas also show up along some Scandinavian and Russian coasts.

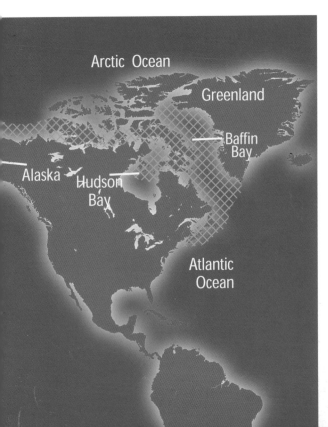

During the winter, belugas migrate to more southern waters. In the springtime, when the ice has melted, they return to the Arctic.

In the springtime, the southernmost parts of the Arctic ice pack begin to melt. Most belugas move north along with the melting ice. This movement is called migration. Pods in the Bering Sea migrate through the Bering Strait to the Chukchi Sea. Other pods shift to far northern Scandinavian islands, upper Baffin Bay near Greenland, or other cooler locations. A migrating pod travels up to a hundred miles each day. Some pods travel as many as fifteen hundred miles to reach their northern ranges.

Some beluga populations do not migrate. Belugas in Alaska's Cook Inlet and Canada's St. Lawrence River **estuary**, for example, stay put all year long. They have everything they need. They

A small group of belugas is encircled by ice. Belugas usually avoid the ice and other Arctic conditions by migrating south for the winter.

do not have to go anywhere when the seasons change.

No matter what time of year it is, most belugas make their homes in shallow waters. In fact, beluga whales often enter water so shallow that it barely covers their bodies. Because of this habit, belugas sometimes get stuck out of the water when the tide goes out. Since belugas breathe air, getting stuck is usually not a problem. A stranded beluga will just relax. It waits for the tide to come back in so it can re-enter the water.

Mating and Birth

Springtime is not only a time for migration. It is also a time for mating. Mating takes place between March and May, and it usually happens in bays and estuaries. With luck, a mating will cause a female to become pregnant. Beluga whales usually carry just one baby, called a **calf**, at a time; twins are rare. The calf grows inside the mother's body for fourteen to fifteen months, which means that calves are born in the summertime the year after a mating.

When a beluga whale is ready to give birth, she swims to warm, shallow waters along a coast or in an estuary. She wriggles and spins her body to force the calf out. Most calves are born tail first. They usually weigh about 150 pounds and are about five feet long. A newborn calf is pink at first but quickly changes to a blue or brownish-red color.

Beluga calves are born knowing how to swim. Within a few seconds of its birth, a newborn calf begins swimming toward the surface to take its first breath. The mother helps the calf by pushing it upward with her flippers.

The Early Years

A newborn calf stays close to its mother at all times. The mother protects the calf. She also feeds it a rich milk that is produced inside her body. The calf sucks the milk from nipples that are hidden in slits along the mother's belly.

Beluga milk contains a lot of fat. This fat helps the baby to form the blubber layer it needs to stay warm in the cold waters of its home. It also gives the baby the energy it needs to grow bigger and stronger.

A beluga calf has no teeth, so it cannot eat solid food at first. It eats only its mother's milk for the first year of life. During the second year, a beluga calf's teeth emerge. The calf then starts eating some solid materials in addition to the milk. A young beluga gradually eats more and more solid food and less and less milk.

Sometime between one and a half and two years of age, a beluga whale is weaned. This means it no longer drinks its mother's milk. The young whale can now take care of itself. It may leave its mother and go to live with another pod.

Growing Up

While it lives with its mother, a calf's skin stays dark. But the skin begins to change color around the time a calf strikes out on its own. It gradually lightens over a period of several years. By the time a beluga is five or six years old, its skin is creamy white. The last parts to lighten are the tail flukes, which may bear gray spots long after the rest of the body has turned white.

Lightening skin is a sign that a beluga whale is reaching maturity. Reaching maturity means that a beluga is able to have babies of its own. Females usually reach this point sometime between four and seven years of age. Males take a little longer; they usually become mature when they are eight or nine years old.

After reaching maturity, males start trying to find mates. They may not succeed right away, however. A male may be physically ready to mate for several years before he gets big enough and strong

A beluga calf swims alongside its mother.

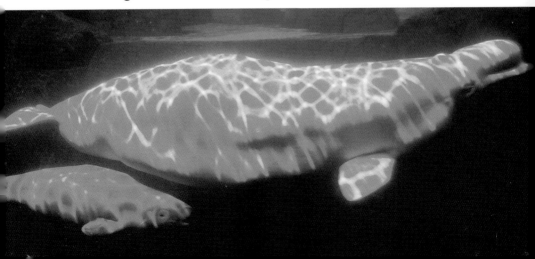

The color of a beluga's tail flukes helps indicate its age. The flukes turn completely white during the whale's fifth or sixth year.

enough to attract females. Once he is able to find mates, he will mate every year for the rest of his life.

Females, on the other hand, start mating as soon as they mature. They mate only in years when they are not pregnant. A female beluga whale usually has one calf every two to three years after she reaches maturity. These babies stay with their mothers for a while and then leave to start their own families—just like their parents before them.

3

Sea Canaries

Belugas are among the most vocal of all whales. They constantly make loud noises that can be heard through the hulls of ships or even out of the water. These noises change from moment to moment and sometimes even sound like songs. Because of this trait, beluga whales are often called "sea canaries." Their singing has delighted sailors since the earliest days of human sea travel.

Today, scientists use waterproof microphones called hydrophones to listen to beluga whales as they chatter in their underwater homes. Hydrophones let scientists hear whales that are far away. They also allow scientists to record beluga songs and study them later. By doing this, scientists hope to learn more about beluga whales.

The Singing Beluga

Belugas can make many sounds. Their calls have been described as barks, chirps, gurgles, grunts, groans, mews, moos, squeaks, trills, whistles, and yaps. Different sounds seem to be used in different situations. Squawks and buzzing noises, for instance, are used mostly during socializing. Sharp grunts are used by mother belugas to warn their calves of danger. The calves respond with whistles. A sharp bang that sounds a little like a human hand clap is an aggressive noise meant to startle other animals. And trilling noises may be used to coordinate movements among a group of belugas.

Besides their natural sounds, beluga whales can also imitate the sounds made by people and other animals. They are very good at this. A beluga whale named Logosi who lived at the Vancouver Aquarium in Canada even learned to say his own name.

Beluga whales respond to each other's noises, so the beluga's song is definitely a form of communication. It is not a language in the human sense, however. Belugas are not using words when they sing to each other. Rather, they are using different sounds to communicate information about their location, mood, and other general concepts.

Making the Sounds

Beluga whales do not have vocal cords, as most mammals do. Instead, they create their songs by moving air between sacs near the blowhole. As the air moves from sac to sac, it is forced through the "lips" of the sacs. The air vibrates the lips as it passes, and these vibrations produce noise. The lips can open and close to change the type of vibrations—and therefore noises—that are being produced.

Once vibrations have been produced, they pass through an organ called the **melon**. The melon, located inside the beluga's head, is a fatty ball that contains oils

Using a complex system of muscles, oil, and air sacs, belugas are able to make a variety of noises to communicate.

of different thicknesses. It is this organ that gives the beluga's forehead its rounded appearance.

As it makes sounds, a beluga whale uses muscles in its head to change the shape of the melon. Doing this changes the oils a noise must pass through. It also changes the melon's thickness. Both of these changes affect the noise being made. A beluga has excellent control over its melon and can make tiny changes to fine-tune its vocalizations. This skill lets beluga whales make the enormous variety of sounds for which they are known.

Changes in the melon can be seen from the outside of the body. When a beluga whale sings, its

The beluga's lower jawbone senses echoes in the water, helping the whale locate objects in the dark.

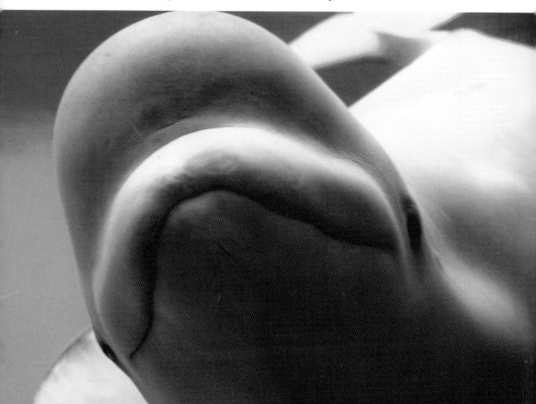

forehead constantly changes shape. These changes make the whale's face look unusually expressive.

Echolocation

Beluga whales use sound for more than just communication. They also use sound to find their way around and to locate objects. Using sound in this way is called **echolocation**. Echolocation is an ability the beluga shares with other toothed whales as well as some out-of-the-water creatures including bats, shrews, and some birds and insects.

To echolocate, a beluga whale produces a rapid series of clicks. The clicks pass through the melon, which focuses the sounds into a beam. The beluga shoots this sound beam forward into the water. The sounds bounce off objects in front of the beluga whale. Some of them are reflected back toward the beluga, which picks up the echoes with its lower jawbone. The echoes are then sent to the brain to be translated into information.

This translation is based on several things. The beluga's brain calculates how long the echo took to return. This tells the beluga how far away an object is. Tiny differences between the original calls and the way the echoes sound tell the whale about an object's shape and texture. Information about an object's size and movements can also be learned through echoes. Taken together, these pieces of information are so good that a beluga can probably

Echolocation

1 *Through echolocation, the beluga whale can "see" with its ears. The whale sends out sound waves.*

2 *The sound waves hit objects such as obstacles and other sea creatures, and bounce back towards the whale.*

3 *The whale receives the returning sound waves with information about the object's size and location.*

"see" with sound nearly as well as a person can see with his or her eyes.

Staying Safe

Echolocation does more than help beluga whales to identify objects. It also helps belugas to avoid trouble in their underwater homes. In particular, belugas use echolocation to find open water above their heads when they are diving. Beluga whales spend a great deal of time swimming beneath ice chunks and vast sheets of ice. Since these animals must come to the water's surface to breathe, the ability to find holes in the ice is important to their safety.

Sound is important to a beluga's safety in other ways, too. Beluga whales use their sensitive hearing

Belugas rely on their hearing to locate dangerous predators and other threats.

to stay away from danger. One scientist experimented with this behavior when he dipped his foot into the water near a group of belugas. Although the closest whales were about a hundred feet away, they heard the noise made by the scientist's foot. They immediately swam away from the scientist. The whales did not leave the area, but they did put a safe distance between themselves and the human intruder.

Beluga whales also use their hearing to avoid killer whales. Killer whales sometimes attack belugas, so beluga whales stay far away from these animals whenever possible. In some areas, crews of fishing boats play recorded killer-whale sounds to scare belugas away. They do this because beluga whales eat the animals the fishing crews are trying to catch. When belugas hear the recorded killer-whale sounds, they think danger is near, so they keep their distance from the fishing boats.

Between their excellent hearing and their amazing vocal abilities, beluga whales depend on sound to live their everyday lives. They also enchant human listeners and provide many fascinating research opportunities for scientists. It is no wonder these "sea canaries" are among the most popular creatures in the world's oceans.

chapter

4

Belugas as Predators and Prey

Beluga whales are **predators**. This means they hunt and eat other animals. To stay healthy, a beluga must eat about 3 percent of its body weight each day. Depending on a whale's weight, 3 percent could be as much as a hundred pounds! In order to find this much food, a beluga spends a great deal of time hunting.

Luckily, beluga whales are not picky eaters. These whales are known to eat about a hundred different species of animals, including fish, octopuses, squid, crabs, shrimp, clams, and sea snails. Between all these prey sources, a beluga whale easily finds and catches the food it needs to survive.

Finding Food

Belugas feed during dives. Feeding dives are usually between two and five minutes long. During a feeding dive, a beluga travels as much as one and a half miles and may dive as deep as two thousand feet. Such deep dives, however, are rare. Belugas prefer to feed in waters no deeper than a hundred feet. As a result, beluga whales usually feed near the shore or where rivers empty into the sea.

Belugas may find food either in open water or by **foraging** along the bottom of the ocean. Open-water meals include fish, squid, and other swimming creatures. Foraged meals include octopuses,

Belugas usually hunt alone. They stick to waters near the shore or the mouth of a river.

worms, and other bottom dwellers. Echolocation is used to find prey both in the open water and on the ocean floor.

When foraging, a beluga whale must sometimes uncover buried prey. To do this, a beluga blows a jet of water out of its mouth at the ocean floor to blast away any material covering a prey animal. A beluga can also use suction to pull a creature from its hiding place.

Beluga whales usually hunt by themselves. Sometimes, however, several belugas dive together and hunt as a group. They herd schools of fish into shallow water, where the fish have less room to escape the hungry whales. The belugas then attack the fish as a group.

Catching and Eating

After a beluga whale finds food, it must catch it. The beluga's flexible neck is a big help in this process. Because beluga whales can move their heads up and down and from side to side, they can react quickly to fast-moving prey. They do not have to turn their bodies around to follow fleeing animals, as other whales do. The ability to move the head is especially important when a beluga is chasing swimming prey, which may be speedy.

Once they get their heads into position, beluga whales use their teeth to grab prey. Belugas have from sixteen to twenty large, rounded teeth in both

The killer whale's impressive size and speed make it a fearsome predator of the beluga.

their upper and lower jaws. The teeth are not sharp enough to spear prey, but they are excellent for grasping and tearing. Using its teeth, a beluga easily rips large prey into bite-size chunks before gobbling it down. Smaller prey is swallowed whole.

When a beluga whale is foraging for food along the ocean floor, it sometimes gets a mouthful of debris along with its meal. Tree bark, plants, stones, and other nonfood materials have been found in the stomachs of beluga whales. This debris does not seem to bother the whale. It passes through the beluga's system without being digested.

Natural Enemies

Most predators become prey for other animals from time to time, and beluga whales are no exception. Although these creatures have few natural enemies, they do sometimes become meals. The main predators of beluga whales are killer whales and polar bears.

Killer whales are much bigger than belugas. They are also much faster. Beluga whales are fairly slow animals, usually swimming at speeds between two and five miles per hour. In an emergency, a beluga can swim as quickly as fifteen miles per hour for short bursts. This is no match for the killer

A polar bear waits for a beluga to surface before reaching into the water for the kill.

whale, however, which can easily reach a speed of thirty miles per hour. If a beluga meets up with a killer whale, there is little it can do to keep itself from being eaten.

Polar bears have a different way of catching beluga whales. They hunt belugas mostly when winter approaches. At this time of year, belugas may get cut off from the open sea by growing ice packs. Sometimes belugas become trapped in a very small area of open water. When the whales surface to breathe, they are close enough to the edge of the ice to be attacked by a waiting polar bear. The polar bear uses its sharp teeth and claws to tear open the beluga's blowhole. This makes it impossible for the whale to go underwater without drowning. The injured beluga is stuck at the surface, where it is easy pickings for the hungry polar bear.

The Impact of Beluga Hunting

Humans are another serious predator of beluga whales. Since ancient times, peoples in Canada, Alaska, and Russia have hunted belugas. In the earliest days, beluga flesh was made into a food called **muktuk**. Beluga skin was also turned into a tough leather. These practices did not hurt beluga populations, since people killed only as many whales as they needed to survive.

Starting in the eighteenth century, however, Europeans and Americans began hunting belugas for commercial sale. Beluga meat, blubber, and melon oil were sold at markets. This caused the number of beluga whales in the world to dip sharply. By the early 1900s, commercial hunting had had a severe effect on beluga populations.

By the mid-1900s, people knew something had to be done to protect beluga whales and other threatened species. In 1972, a law called the Marine Mammal Protection Act made it illegal to hunt any marine mammal, including beluga whales, in U.S. waters. And in 1973, the Convention on International Trade in Endangered Species (CITES) was created to monitor human treatment of toothed whales and other species. Together, these acts greatly reduced the hunting of beluga whales.

For over two hundred years, commercial hunters sought belugas for their meat, blubber, and oil.

Beluga Hunting Today

But beluga whales are still killed by humans. Illegal hunting and bycatch (accidentally killing one animal while hunting for another) affect the entire range of belugas. And hunting is still legal for Native Americans in the United States and Canada. In total, this group kills an estimated fifteen hundred beluga whales each year for their flesh and melon oil.

Belugas in some areas are also affected by human pollution. The beluga population in Canada's St. Lawrence River, for example, is known to suffer from poisoning, tumors, and other deadly health problems. Belugas in other areas can also be harmed by the poisons people dump into the world's seas.

Hunting and pollution have reduced the number of belugas in the world. At this time, belugas do not seem to be in danger of extinction. But the World Conservation Union, an organization that keeps track of the world's species, places beluga whales in the "insufficiently known" category. This means belugas are suspected of being either endangered, threatened, or vulnerable. Scientists and concerned citizens must keep a careful watch on the world's beluga whale population to make sure these remarkable animals continue to thrive.

Glossary

blow: The cloud of seawater, water vapor, and stale air exhaled by a beluga whale.

blowhole: A hole on the head through which the beluga whale breathes.

blubber: A thick layer of fat that lies just beneath the beluga whale's skin.

calf: A baby beluga whale.

cetacean: The name of the family to which all whales, dolphins, and porpoises belong.

dorsal ridge: A bony, bumpy spine along the beluga whale's back.

echolocation: The ability to "see" with sound. Sound waves are sent out and the returning echoes are interpreted.

estuary: A region of semi-salty water where a river runs into an ocean.

flukes: Flattened pads of tough tissue at the end of the beluga whale's tail.

forage: To search for food along the bottom of the ocean.

marine mammal: A mammal that lives in an ocean environment.

melon: An oil-filled organ in a beluga whale's head that changes and directs sound waves.

migration: Traveling every year from one place to another along a similar route.

molting: The annual shedding of skin.

muktuk: A food consisting of strips of whale skin with blubber attached.

pod: A group of whales.

predator: Any animal that hunts other animals for food.

spyhopping: Poking the head out of the water to look around.

For Further Exploration

Books

Mark Carwardine, Erich Hoyt, R. Ewan Fordyce, and Peter Gill, *Whales, Dolphins and Porpoises.* Alexandria, VA: Nature Company/Time-Life, 1998. Includes lots of good information about beluga whales and other cetacean species.

Tony Martin, *Beluga Whales.* Stillwater, MN: Voyageur Press, 1996. This general reference includes extra information and stories for slightly more advanced readers.

Kenneth S. Norris, "Beluga: White Whale of the North," *National Geographic*, June 1994. The author tells of his travels to the Canadian Arctic where he visited scientists who were studying beluga whales.

Brian Skerry, *A Whale on Her Own: The True Story of Wilma the Beluga Whale.* Woodbridge, CT: Blackbirch Press, Inc., 2000. This is the true story of the author's friendship with Wilma, a beluga whale living in Canada's Chedabucto Bay.

Websites

Beluga Whale (www.enchantedlearning.com).
This general reference site includes links to beluga
whale word searches, connect-the-dots puzzles,
and other activities for kids.

Sound Recordings

Echoes of Nature: Beluga Whales. Delta, 1995.
This CD is a collection of beluga whale songs
recorded in the wild.

picture credits

about the author

Kris Hirschmann has written more than seventy books for children. She is the president of The Wordshop, a business that provides a wide variety of writing and editorial services. She holds a bachelor's degree in psychology from Dartmouth College in Hanover, New Hampshire. Hirschmann lives just outside of Orlando, Florida, with her husband, Michael, and her daughter, Nikki.